LAUGHTER
Therapy

BOB PHILLIPS
& JONNY HAWKINS

HARVEST HOUSE PUBLISHERS
EUGENE, OREGON

Cover design by Studio Gearbox

Interior design by KUHN Design Group

Cover photo © Iliveinoctober, LineTale / Shutterstock

For bulk, special sales, or ministry purchases, please call 1-800-547-8979.
Email: customerservice@hhpbooks.com

M is a federally registered trademark of the Hawkins Children's LLC. Harvest House Publishers, Inc., is the exclusive licensee of the trademark.

Laughter Therapy
Copyright © 2021 text by Bob Phillips. Artwork by Jonny Hawkins
Published by Harvest House Publishers
Eugene, Oregon 97408
www.harvesthousepublishers.com

ISBN 978-0-7369-8317-4 (pbk)
ISBN 978-0-7369-8318-1 (eBook)

Library of Congress Control Number: 2021930674

Printed in the United States of America

21 22 23 24 25 26 27 28 29 / BP / 10 9 8 7 6 5 4 3 2 1

ABALONE

An expression of disbelief.

ACCIDENT

After an accident, an elderly woman stepped forward and prepared to help the victim. She was asked to step aside by a man who announced:

"Everyone step back, please! I've had a course in first aid, and I'm trained in CPR!"

The older woman watched what he did for a few minutes. Then she tapped him on the shoulder.

"When you get to the part about calling a doctor," she said. "I'm already here."

ACCOUNTANTS

The company accountant is shy and retiring. He's shy a quarter of a million dollars. That's why he's retiring.

———

Q: What's an accountant's idea of trashing his or her hotel room?
A: Refusing to fill out the guest comment card.

———

Q: Why do some accountants decide to become actuaries?
A: They find bookkeeping too exciting.

ACHES AND PAINS

I've got so many aches and pains that if a new one comes today, it will be at least two weeks before I can worry about it.

ACQUAINTANCE

A person you know well enough to borrow money from but not well enough to lend money to.

ACUPUNCTURE

There must be something to acupuncture—you never see any sick porcupines.

ADVICE

"Be yourself" is the worst advice you can give some people.

———

Socrates was a Greek philosopher who went around giving good advice. They poisoned him.

———

It's surprising how many people will unselfishly neglect their own work in order to tell you how to do yours.

"Oops, my pen leaked. Tell me,
Dr. Stratton…what do you see?"

Mood swings

ALARM CLOCK

An alarm clock is a strange device that
makes people rise and whine.

AMBITION

Some folks can look so busy doing nothing
that they seem indispensable.

ANDY

A little boy came home from Sunday school and told his mother they
had just learned a new song about a boy named Andy. His mother
couldn't understand what he meant until he sang:

Andy walks with me,
Andy talks with me,
Andy tells me I am His own.

ANGER

A young girl who was writing a paper for school came to her father and
asked, "Dad, what is the difference between anger and exasperation?"

The father replied, "It is mostly a matter of degree. Let me show you
what I mean." With that the father pulled out his phone and dialed
a number at random. To the man who answered the phone, he said,
"Hello, is Melvin there?" The man answered, "There's no one living here
named Melvin. Why don't you look up numbers before you dial them?"

"See," said the father to his daughter. "That man was not a bit happy
with our call. He was probably very busy with something, and we
annoyed him. Now watch…"

The father dialed the number again, "Hello, is Melvin there?" asked
the father.

"Now look here!" came the heated reply, "You just called this number, and I told you that there is no Melvin here! You've got a lot of nerve calling again!" He slammed the receiver down hard.

The father turned to his daughter and said, "You see, that was anger. Now I'll show you what exasperation means." He again dialed the same number, and when a violent voice roared, "Hello!" the father calmly said, "Hello, this is Melvin. Have there been any calls for me?"

APPEAL

What a banana comes in.

ARMY

The first sergeant was holding a class on combat for his company. He said, "Jones, what would you do if you saw 700 enemy soldiers coming straight at you?"

Jones said, "I would shoot them all with my rifle."

The sergeant asked, "What if on the right you saw 400 enemy soldiers charging you? What would you do?"

Jones said, "I would shoot them with my rifle."

The sergeant continued, "Okay! Then on your left, Jones, you notice 1,000 enemy soldiers honing in on you. What would you do?"

Jones answered again, "I would shoot them all."

The sergeant yelled, "Just a minute, Jones. Where are you getting all those bullets?"

The soldier smiled and said, "The same place you're getting all of those enemy soldiers."

"I keep forgetting to read my
self-motivational books."

ASTRONAUT

The astronaut preparing for his moon launch was being interviewed by the press. "How do you feel?" asked one reporter.

"How would you feel if you were going to the moon in a vehicle with over 150,000 parts and you knew they were all supplied by the lowest bidder?"

AUCTIONEER

The auctioneer interrupted his chanting to announce that someone in the crowd had lost a billfold containing $1,000 and was offering a $200 reward for its return.

A voice from the rear of the crowd piped up, "I bid $210."

BABY

An alimentary canal with a loud voice at one
end and no responsibility at the other.

BABYSITTER

Someone you employ to watch your television set.

BAD LANGUAGE

An elderly lady was shocked by the language used by two men repairing telephone wires near her home. She wrote a letter to the company complaining. The foreman was ordered to report the happenings to his superior. "Me and Joe Wilson were on this job," he reported. "I was up on the telephone pole, and I accidentally let hot lead fall on Joe, and it went down his neck. Then he called up to me, 'You really must be more careful, Harry.'"

"How does that make you feel?"

BEASTLY WEATHER

Raining cats and dogs.

BEE

Woman: One of your bees just stung me. I want you to do something about it.

Beekeeper: Certainly, madam. Just show me which bee it was, and I'll have it punished.

BEHAVIOR

Father: Do you think it will improve Junior's behavior if we buy him a bicycle?

Mother: No, but it'll spread it over a wider area.

BEHOLD

What one bee wrestler uses to pin another bee wrestler.

BENEFITS OF GROWING OLDER

- You can eat dinner at 4:00 p.m.
- Your eyes won't get much worse.
- Things you buy now won't wear out.
- Kidnappers are not very interested in you.
- People no longer view you as a hypochondriac.
- No one expects you to run into a burning building.
- You enjoy hearing arguments about pension plans.

- You no longer think of speed limits as a challenge.
- Your supply of brain cells is finally down to a manageable size.
- Your investment in health insurance is finally beginning to pay off.
- Your secrets are safe with your friends because they can't remember them.
- Your joints are a more accurate meteorologist than the National Weather Service.

BILL

Wife: A man at the door wants to see you about a bill you owe. He wouldn't give his name.

Husband: What does he look like?

Wife: He looks like you had better pay him.

BIRTHSTONE

Son: Dad, this magazine article says that my birthstone is the ruby. What is yours?

Father: The grindstone.

BORE

Mark Twain was once trapped by a bore who lectured to him about the hereafter: "Do you realize that every time I exhale, some poor soul leaves this world and passes on to the great beyond?"

"Really? Why don't you try chewing cloves?"

"I think the surgery went well, especially considering I'm a doctor of literature."

Anger Management Clinic

"Ten forty-five for me—when's your teed off time?"

At a formal dinner, the hostess, who was seated at the far end of the table from a very famous actress, wrote a note to the actress and had the butler deliver it.

The actress couldn't read without her glasses, so she asked the man at her left to read it to her. "It says," he began, "'Dear, do me a favor and please don't neglect the man at your left. I know he's a bore but talk to him.'"

BRACES

Is it true that getting braces for your children is
putting your money where your mouth is?

BREATH

Husband: This report says that every time I breathe, three Chinese people die.

Wife: That doesn't surprise me. You've got to stop eating so much garlic.

BULLETS

Q: What happens when two bullets get married?

A: They have a little BB.

BURNED OUT

Show me a burned-out post office,
and I'll show you a case of blackmail.

CACKLING

A clergyman had been invited to attend a party of the Sunday school nursery department. He decided to surprise them, so getting on his hands and knees, flapping his coat tails over his head like wings, he hopped in on all fours, cackling like a bird. Imagine his surprise when he learned that due to a switch in locations, he had intruded on the ladies' missionary meeting!

CAMEL

Q: What do you call a camel without a hump?

A: Humphrey.

CANNIBAL

"Tell me," the missionary asked a cannibal, "do you think religion has made any headway here?"

"Yes," answered the native. "Now we only eat fishermen on Fridays."

CARDS

A man walked by a table in a hotel and noticed three men and a dog playing cards. The dog was playing with extraordinary performance.

"This is a very smart dog," the man commented.

"Not so smart," said one of the players. "Every time he gets a good hand, he wags his tail."

CARSICKNESS

The feeling you get every month when the payment is due.

"At times I wonder what I've done with my life that makes me worth saving."

CAT FOOD

A butcher was waiting on one woman when a second woman ran into the shop. "Quick," the second woman said to the butcher, "give me a pound of cat food, will you? Then she turned to the woman who had been ahead of her at the counter. "I hope you don't mind my butting in ahead of you," she said.

"No," said the first woman, "not if you're that hungry."

CENSUS

When the Viking explorer Leif Erikson returned from his New World voyage, he found that his name had been dropped from the registry of his hometown. He reported the omission to the chief town official who, deeming it a slight to a distinguished citizen, protested strongly to the district census taker.

"I'm terribly sorry," apologized the census taker in great embarrassment. "I must have taken Leif off my census."

CENTURION

A Roman who is a hundred years old.

CHAOS

Surgeon: I think the medical profession is the first profession mentioned in the Bible. God made Eve by carving a rib out of Adam.

Engineer: No, engineering was first. Just think of the engineering job it was to create things out of chaos.

Politician: That's nothing...who do you think created chaos?

CHAPPED LIPS

Q: What's worse than a giraffe with a sore throat?

A: A hippopotamus with chapped lips.

CHESS

A group of chess players had congregated in the lobby of a big New York hotel. Each person tried to outdo the other in tales of his prowess in mastering opponents. After a while, the hotel manager shouted, "Everybody out!"

Asked why, he said, "I can't stand chess nuts boasting in an open foyer."

CHILDREN

Mother: Suzie, what have you been doing this morning while I was working in the kitchen?

Suzie: I was playing postman.

Mother: How could you play postman when you don't have any letters?

Suzie: I was looking through your trunk in the garage and found a packet of letters tied with a nice ribbon, and I posted one in everyone's mailbox on the block.

———

Children keep the family together—
especially if you can't find a babysitter.

"No, it's not about lost sheep.
Something's got my goat."

CHIMNEY SWEEP

Person who does things to soot himself.

CHOIR

John: What made you give up singing in the choir?

Jack: I was absent one Sunday, and someone asked if the organ had been fixed.

CHURCH

Some go to church to take a walk;
Some go there to laugh and talk;
Some go there to meet a friend;
Some go there their time to spend;
Some go there to meet a lover;
Some go there a fault to cover;
Some go there for speculation;
Some go there for observation;
Some go there to doze and nod;
The wise go there to worship God.

———

Wife: Did you see that hat Mrs. Jones wore to church?

Husband: No!

Wife: Did you see the new dress Mrs. Smith had on?

Husband: No!

Wife: A lot of good it does you to go to church!

COLLEGE

"Has your son's college education been of any tangible value?" inquired a friend.

"Oh yes. For one thing, it completely cured his mother of bragging about him."

COLLEGE GRADUATE

A young man hired by a large supermarket chain reported to work at one of the stores. The manager greeted him with a smile, handed him a broom, and said, "Your first job will be to sweep out the store."

"But," the young man said, "I'm a college graduate."

"I'm sorry. I didn't know that," said the manager. "Give me the broom, and I'll show you how."

COMMITTEE

A certain congregation was about to erect a new church edifice. The building committee, in consecutive meetings, passed the fellowship resolutions:

1. We shall build a new church.

2. The new building is to be located on the site of the old one.

3. The material in the old building is to be used in the new one.

4. We shall continue to use the old building until the new one is completed.

"Poor Sigmund.
Mrs. Freud gave him the slip."

"I shouldn't eat it, but I'm a gluten for punishment."

COMMUTER

At a commuter train station a policeman noticed a woman driver bowed over the steering wheel of her car in evident discomfort.

"Is there anything wrong?" asked the policeman.

Half crying and half laughing, the woman responded, "For ten years I have driven my husband to the station to catch his train. This morning I forgot him!"

COMPLAINT

Customer in restaurant: I'll have some raw oysters, not too small, not too salty or too fat. They must be cold, and I want them quickly!

Waiter: Yes, sir. With or without pearls?

CONGRATULATIONS

"Dear Emily, words cannot express how much I regret having broken off our engagement. Will you please come back to me? Your absence leaves a space no one can fill. Please forgive me and let us start all over again. I need you so much.

Yours forever, Bob.

P.S. By the way, congratulations on winning the state lottery."

CONGRESS

There are two periods when Congress does no business—one is before the holidays, and the other is after.

———

A congressman recently hired a dozen research
assistants—one to dig up the facts, and the
other 11 to bury them as deeply as possible.

————

What this country needs is more unemployed politicians.

————

I could study all my life and not think up half the amount
of funny things they think of in one session of Congress.

WILL ROGERS

————

Fleas can be taught nearly anything that a congressman can.

MARK TWAIN

————

In biblical times it took a divine act for a donkey
to speak. Unfortunately, many in Congress
exercise this miracle power every day.

————

Congress is where a person gets up to speak, says
nothing, and nobody listens. Then everyone
rises in disagreement with what's been said.

————

"I can never be as fit as a fiddle."

"He's an infectiologist and she's an epidemiologist—
they had a few bugs in their relationship."

Congress just voted themselves another pay raise, saying it would motivate them to be more productive.

———

There are only three ways to become a millionaire: inherit money, start a business and work hard, or get elected to Congress.

———

You can lead a man to Congress, but you can't make him think.

CONSCIENCE

Mark Twain used to tell the story of how he once stole a watermelon from a cart when the owner was not looking. He carried the melon to a secret spot, sat down, and was just about to bite into the melon when he realized that he should not do that. It just wasn't right.

So he got up, took the watermelon back, replaced it on the cart, and took a ripe one.

COVID–19

So many coronavirus jokes out there—it's a pundemic.

———

Did you hear the about the cure for coronavirus? It's a riot.

———

What should you do if you don't understand
a coronavirus joke. Be patient.

————

Since the coronavirus health crisis, we'll be
making only inside jokes from now on.

————

I'll tell you a coronavirus joke now, but you'll
have to wait two weeks to see if you got it.

————

Because of coronavirus, nail salons, hair salons,
beauty parlors, waxing centers, and tanning places
are closed. It's ugly out there, people.

————

I've got to be clear about home-schooling during
the coronavirus pandemic: I'm not really talking to
myself…I'm having a parent-teacher conference.

————

My mother told me I wouldn't accomplish anything
by lying in bed all day. But look at me now! I'm
saving the world from the coronavirus.

————

Whose idea was it to sing "Happy Birthday" while washing your
hands? Now every time I go to the bathroom, my kids expect me to
walk out with a cake and candles.

————

"No wonder he's so testy."

The World Health Organization (WHO) announced that dogs cannot contract the coronavirus. Dogs previously held in quarantine can now be released. To be clear, WHO let the dogs out!

———

My husband purchased a world map and then gave me a dart and said, "Throw it, and wherever it lands—that's where I'm taking you when this pandemic ends." Turns out, we're spending two weeks behind the fridge.

———

The coronavirus is really keeping people at home. I saw my neighbor sitting on her porch talking to her cat. It was obvious she thought her cat understood her. I then went inside my house and told my dog about it—we laughed a lot.

———

Knock, knock.

Who's there?

Coronavirus.

Seriously! Don't touch my door! Put on your mask! And socially distance six feet! And now I have to sanitize the door because of you! Thanks a lot!

COW

Q: Where do you get dragon milk?

A: From a cow with short legs!

COWBOYS

Minister before the morning offering: The Lord owns the cattle on a thousand hills. He only needs cowboys to round them up. Will the ushers please come forward for the offering?

CRAZY THOUGHTS

Is it only me—or do buffalo wings taste just like chicken?

———

A procrastinator's job is never done.

———

I tried to drown my thoughts, but they learned to swim.

———

Q: What do you call a dinosaur with an extensive vocabulary?
A: A thesaurus.

———

Did you ever notice? "The" and "IRS"
put together spells "theirs"?

———

I used to wish I could read minds. Then I got
a Facebook account, and now I'm over it.

———

The sole purpose of a child's middle name is
so he can tell when he's really in trouble.

———

Why is it that insurance people always
talk about death benefits?

———

It's so simple to be wise. Just think of
something stupid to say and don't say it.

Sam Levenson

CREDIT CARDS

Life was simpler before credit cards. You didn't have to wait until the end of the month to find out how poor you were.

CRIMINALS

A candidate for the police force was being verbally examined. "If you were by yourself in a police car and were pursued by a desperate gang of criminals in another car doing 40 miles an hour along a lonely road, what would you do?"

The candidate looked puzzled for a moment. Then he replied, "Fifty."

CRITICISM

Pay no attention to what critics say. There has
never been a statue set up in honor of a critic.

"It's hard to think about eternal life...
during prime time."

COUNTERFEIT

A seizure while paying your bill at the supermarket.

DAFFY DICTIONARY

Accordion—a bagpipe with pleats.

Archive—where Noah kept his bees.

Barium—what we do to most people when they die.

Baseball—12 minutes of excitement crammed into two and a half hours.

Bore—a man who, when asked how he is, tells you.

Budget—a family's attempt to live below its yearnings.

Business Meeting—a time for a group of people to get together and talk about what they're supposed to be doing.

Committee—a group of the unwilling, chosen from the unfit, to do the unnecessary.

Consultant—someone who takes the watch off your wrist and tells you the time.

Dermatologist—one who makes rash statements.

Desk—a wastebasket with drawers.

Diet—a short period of starvation followed by a rapid gain of five pounds.

Diplomacy—the art of letting someone else have your own way.

Egotist—someone who is me-deep in conversation.

Experience—the name people give to their mistakes.

Extradition—more math homework.

Flattery—an insult in gift wrapping.

Geologist—a faultfinder.

Glutton—someone who eats the big slice of cake you wanted.

Gossiper—someone with a lively sense of rumor.

Gross Ignorance—144 times worse than ordinary ignorance.

Hypochondriac—someone who won't let well enough alone.

Jazz—five people on the same stage…all playing a different tune.

Justice—a decision in your favor.

Liability—a talent for lying.

Miser—a person who lets the world go buy.

Monologue—a conversation between a politician and somebody else.

Obstetrician—a doctor making money on the stork market.

Orthopedist—a doctor who gets all the breaks.

Outpatient—a person who has fainted.

Pediatrician—a doctor with little patients.

Pessimist—someone who looks at life through woes-colored glasses.

Pharmacist—a helper on a farm.

Pickpocket—a person who finds things before people lose them.

Polarize—what penguins see with.

Psychiatrist—someone who finds you cracked and leaves you broke.

"I think I'm having a mud-life crisis."

"Working nights doesn't bother me. That's
because I have a sunny disposition."

Refrigerator—a place to store leftovers until they are ready to be thrown out.

Secret—something you tell to one person at a time.

Shin—the human bone most useful for finding hard obstacles in the dark.

Synonym—a word you use when you can't spell the other one.

Tact—changing the subject without changing your mind.

Tomorrow—the day you are going to clean out the garage.

Upgrade—a computer program with new and improved bugs.

Vacuum Cleaner—a broom with a stomach.

Worry—interest paid on trouble before it falls due.

Wrinkles—something other people have. (You have character lines.)

Yawn—an honest opinion openly expressed.

DANDRUFF

Chips off the old block.

DATE

"I just had a date with a pair of Siamese twins."

"Did you have a good time?"

"Yes and no."

DEER

Q: What do you call a deer with no eyes?

A: No eye deer.

DEPENDS

"How late do you usually sleep on Sunday morning?"

"It all depends."

"Depends on what?"

"The length of the sermon."

DIAGNOSIS

A doctor was called in to see a very busy patient. "Well, sir, what's the matter?" he asked cheerfully.

"That's for you to find out," the patient snapped.

"I see," said the doctor. "Well, if you'll excuse me a minute, I'll phone a friend of mine…a veterinarian. He's the only man I know who can make a diagnosis without asking questions."

DIET

Did you hear about the garlic and Limburger cheese diet? You don't lose any weight, but your friends will think you look thinner from a distance.

DIETING

Triumph of mind over platter.

"Every so often I get this overwhelming
fear of wide-open spaces."

"My client, Mr. Shep, is charging your client,
Ms. Mittens, with alienation of affection."

DIFFERENCE

Q: What is the difference between the North and South Pole?

A: All the difference in the world.

DINNER SPEAKER

A dinner speaker was in such a hurry to get to his engagement that when he arrived and sat down at the head table, he suddenly realized that he had forgotten his false teeth.

Turning to the man next to him he said, "I forgot my teeth." The man said, "No problem." With that he reached into his pocket and pulled out a pair of false teeth. "Try these," he said. The speaker tried them. "Too loose," he said. The man then said, "I have another pair—try these." The speaker tried them and responded, "Too tight." The man was not taken back at all. He then said, "I have one more pair of false teeth—try them." The speaker said, "They fit perfectly." With that he ate his meal and gave his address.

After the dinner meeting was over, the speaker went over to thank the man who had helped him.

"I want to thank you for coming to my aid. Where is your office? I've been looking for a good dentist." The man replied, "I'm not a dentist. I'm an undertaker."

DIRTY

Q: If a man crosses the ocean twice without taking a bath, what is he called?

A: A dirty double crosser.

DISTURB

"Young man," said the angry father from the head of the stairs, "didn't I hear the clock strike four when you brought my daughter in?"

"You did," admitted the boyfriend. "It was going to strike eleven, but I grabbed it and held the gong so it wouldn't disturb you."

The father muttered, "Doggone! Why didn't I think of that one in my dating days!"

DOCTOR

Patient: Doctor, is there anything you can do to cure my snoring?

Doctor: Does it disturb your wife?

Patient: No, it only embarrasses my wife. It is the rest of the people in the church that are disturbed.

———

Did you hear about the man who complained that every time he put on his hat he heard music? The doctor fixed him up. He removed the hat band.

———

Friend: How is your new "doctor" son getting along in his practice?

Mother: Fine. He is doing so well he can occasionally tell a patient there is nothing the matter with him.

———

"You're shedding and rolling over
'cuz you're sick as a dog."

"Argh! A whole plate of sushi!
What do you have—a hollow leg?"

Doctor, Doctor, I feel like a sheep.

That's baaaaaaaaaad!

———

Doctor, Doctor, I feel like a dog.

Sit.

———

Doctor, Doctor, I feel like an apple.

We must get to the core of this.

———

Doctor, Doctor, everyone keeps throwing me in the garbage.

Don't talk rubbish!

———

Doctor, Doctor, how can I cure my sleepwalking?

Sprinkle tacks all over your bedroom floor.

———

Doctor, Doctor, I think I'm a burglar!

Have you taken anything for it?

———

Doctor, Doctor, everyone thinks I'm a liar.

Well, that's hard to believe.

———

Doctor, Doctor, I'm having trouble with my breathing.

I'll give you something that will soon put a stop to that!

———

Doctor, Doctor, what did the X-ray of my head show?

Absolutely nothing!

———

Doctor, Doctor, I feel like a pair of curtains.

Oh, pull yourself together!

———

Doctor, Doctor, I think I'm a rubber band.

Why don't you stretch yourself out on the couch there and tell me all about it.

———

Doctor, Doctor, I've broken my arm in two places.

Well don't go back there again.

———

"I appreciate your devices, which make it seem like
you're paying attention, but could you actually pay
attention and make eye contact so I know you are?"

Doctor, Doctor, I think I'm an electric eel.

That's shocking!

———

Doctor, Doctor, my husband smells like a fish.

Poor sole!

———

Doctor, Doctor, I think I'm a snake about to shed its skin.

Why don't you go behind the screen and slip into something more comfortable!

———

Doctor, Doctor, I've only got 59 seconds to live.

Wait a minute, please.

———

Doctor, Doctor, I think I'm a frog.

What's wrong with that?

I think I'm going to croak!

———

Doctor, Doctor, these pills you gave me for my body odor don't work.

What's wrong with them?

They keep slipping out from under my arms!

———

Doctor, Doctor, you've got to help me. Some mornings I wake up and think I'm Donald Duck. Other times I think I'm Mickey Mouse.

Hmmm. How long have you been having these Disney spells?

———

Doctor, Doctor, I keep thinking I'm a bell.

Take these pills, and if they don't help, give me a ring.

———

Some doctors prefer to tell you the bad news face-to-face. Others are chicken and prefer to send you the bill through the mail.

———

Doctor: Have you ever been troubled by appendicitis?

Patient: Only when I've tried to spell it.

———

Doctor: I'm afraid you're anemic.

Patient: I'd like a second opinion.

Doctor: Okay, you're ugly too.

———

Doctor: If I find the operation necessary, would you have the money to pay for it?

Patient: If I didn't have the money, would you find the operation necessary?

———

Doctor: You've burned both your ears! How did that happen?

Patient: I was ironing when the telephone rang.

Doctor: But how did you burn both of them?

Patient: Well, just as soon as I put the phone down, it rang again.

———

A man went to see his doctor. "Doctor," he said, "my arm keeps talking to me."

"Don't be ridiculous," said the doctor.

"No, really it does. Listen."

So the doctor put his stethoscope to the man's arm and heard the arm say: "Lend me five bucks."

"It's okay," said the doctor. "It's just broke."

———

A doctor's waiting room is a place where
patients test their patience.

———

An apple a day will keep the doctor away...assuming, of course, that it hasn't been grown in chemical soil, sprayed with pesticides, and then covered with wax.

———

Did you hear about the guy whose doctor told him to
go on a liquid diet...so he melted all his ice cream?

DOUGHNUTS

Doctor: Your sign outside says, "Our Doughnuts Have Fewer Calories." I demand to know how you can make doughnuts with fewer calories.

Baker: If you really must know…we make them smaller than anyone else.

DRAMA CRITIC

One who gives the best jeers of his life to the theater.

DRIVE-IN

Have you heard of the new drive-in
confessional? It is called, "Toot and tell."

DULL

One girl to another: "There's never a dull moment when
you're out with Jim—it lasts the whole evening."

ECCENTRIC

Wife: Everyone in church is talking about the quarrel the Joneses have been having. Some are taking her side, and some are taking his.

Husband: And I suppose a few eccentric individuals are minding their own business.

**"It's just until the air conditioning
in our house is fixed."**

"If you really believed in me, you wouldn't
get a second opinion, Mom."

ECHO

First golfer: How many strokes did it take you to get out of that sand trap?

Second golfer: Three.

First golfer: But I heard six.

Second golfer: Three were echoes.

ELECTROCARDIOGRAPH

A ticker tape.

ELEPHANT

Q: How do you make an elephant fly?

A: Well, first you take a grea-a-t big zipper...

———

Q: How did elephants get flat feet?

A: From jumping out of trees.

———

Q: Why is it dangerous to go into the jungle between two and four in the afternoon?

A: Because that's when elephants are jumping out of trees.

Q: Why are pygmies so small?

A: They went into the jungle between two and four in the afternoon.

EMBARRASSED

The young lady eyed her date with great disapproval. "That's the fourth time you've gone back for more ice cream and cake, Albert," she said acidly. "Doesn't it embarrass you at all?"

"Why should it?" The hungry fellow said with a shrug. "I keep telling them I'm getting it for you."

ENDANGERED

One national park ranger to another: What do we do if we see an endangered animal eating an endangered plant?

EUREKA

A euphemism for "You smell bad."

PSYCHOANALYSIS CALIFORNIA STYLE

"You need a bypass. Bypass the buffet
and head to the salad bar."

EXAMPLE

Few things are harder to put up with than
the annoyance of a good example.

MARK TWAIN

EXERCISE

The only exercise some people get is jumping at conclusions, running down their friends, sidestepping responsibility, and pushing their luck.

FAINTED

A man rose from his seat in a crowded bus so a woman standing nearby could sit down. She was so surprised she fainted. When she revived and sat down, she said, "Thanks."

Then the man fainted.

FAMILY

Q: How do you get rid of company that stays too long?

A: Treat them like the rest of the family.

FEET

Q: How many feet are in a yard?

A: It depends on how many people are in the yard.

FILING CABINET

A metal box where you can systematically lose things.

FINE

A fine is a tax for doing wrong. A tax is a fine for doing well.

FIREPROOF

The boss's relatives.

FLIRTING

Peggy: I caught my boyfriend flirting.

Sharon: Yes, that's the way I caught mine too.

FLOODED

Wife: Honey, I can't get the car started. I think it's flooded.

Husband: Where is it?

Wife: In the swimming pool.

"I think you're plum crazy."

"I see by your resume that the voices in
your head recommend you highly."

FLOWERS

First actor: What's the matter with the leading lady?

Second actor: She only got nine bouquets of flowers tonight.

First actor: Good heavens! Isn't that enough?

Second actor: Nope. She paid for ten.

FOOD

Customer: Waiter, there's a fly in my chop suey.

Waiter: That's nothing. Wait until you see what's in your fortune cookie.

————

Young bride: There are two things that I am good at preparing: meatballs and lemon pie.

Young husband: And which one is this?

FOOL

Reverend Henry Ward Beecher received a letter with one word written on it. It said, "Fool." The next Sunday he read the letter from the pulpit and said, "I have received many letters from people who have forgotten to sign their names, but this is the first time I've received a letter from someone who signed his name but forgot to write the letter."

————

Grandfather: Lincoln said, "You can fool all the people some of the time and some of the people all the time."

Grandson: But what happens the rest of the time?

Grandfather: They're likely to make fools of themselves, I reckon.

FOOT

Three rabbits lived together. One was named Foot, the second one Foot Foot, and the third was called Foot Foot Foot.

One day Foot was feeling bad, so Foot Foot and Foot Foot Foot took Foot to a doctor. After examining Foot, the doctor spoke to Foot Foot and Foot Foot Foot.

"I'm afraid there isn't much I can do for your friend," he said. "He's very sick."

Sure enough, after only a week, Foot died, and Foot Foot and Foot Foot Foot were upset. Then one morning the following month Foot Foot said to Foot Foot Foot, "I feel terrible."

So Foot Foot Foot packed up Foot Foot and took him off to another doctor.

"We'll get a good doctor this time," Foot Foot Foot said to Foot Foot. "That last one certainly didn't help Foot."

The new doctor gave Foot Foot a thorough physical examination and reported to Foot Foot Foot that Foot Foot was very ill indeed. Foot Foot Foot became hysterical. "You've just got to save him, doctor! We already have one Foot in the grave!"

"Sure, he's spewing molten lava, but that's just indicative of a much deeper problem."

"Hold on a second while I inflate his ego."

FOREMAN

The news that Bill had lost his job got around quickly, and a friend asked, "Why did the foreman fire you?"

"You know what a foreman is," Bill shrugged. "The one who stands around and watches other men work."

"What's that got to do with it?" his friend wanted to know.

"Well, he just got jealous of me," Bill explained. "Everyone thought I was the foreman."

FORGOTTEN

I'm in a dilemma. I'm having amnesia and déjà vu at the same time. I think I've forgotten this before.

FORMULA

Teacher: What's the formula for water?

Student: *H, I, J, K, L, M, N, O*.

Teacher: That's not the formula I gave you.

Student: Yes, it is. You said it was *H* to *O*.

FRIGHTENED FLOWER ARRANGER

A petrified florist.

FUNERAL

"Do you believe in life after death?" The boss asked one of his younger employees.

"Yes, sir."

"Well, then, that makes everything just fine," the boss went on. "About an hour after you left yesterday to go to your grandfather's funeral, he stopped in to see you."

GARDENER

A good gardener is a handyman with a sense of humus.

GENERATION GAP

You can tell there is a generation gap when a teenager drives his car into the garage and runs over his father's bicycle.

GHOST

Years ago, a photographer went to a haunted castle determined to get a picture of a ghost that was said to appear only once in a hundred years. Not wanting to frighten off the spook, the photographer sat in the dark until midnight when the apparition became visible.

The ghost turned out to be friendly and consented to pose for a snapshot. The happy photographer popped a bulb into his camera and took the picture. Then he dashed to his studio, developed the negative and groaned. It was underexposed and completely blank.

Moral: The spirit was willing, but the flash was weak.

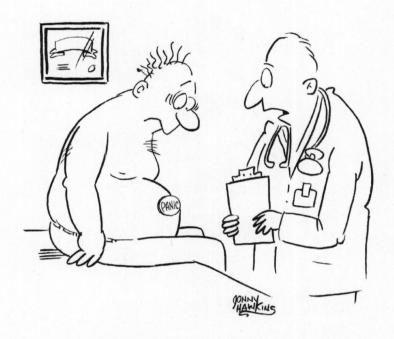

"That would explain the anxiety."

GIVING

Isn't it funny how a $20 can look so big when you take it to church, and so small when you take it to the store?

GOLF

Wife: George, you promised you'd be home at four o'clock. It's now eight.

George: Honey, please listen to me. Poor ol' Fred is dead. He just dropped over on the eighth green.

Wife: Oh, that's awful.

George: It surely was. For the rest of the game, it was hit the ball, drag Fred, hit the ball, drag Fred...

GOOD SAMARITAN

Sunday school teacher: In the story of the Good Samaritan, why did the Levite pass by on the other side of the road?

Student: Because the poor man had already been robbed.

GOSSIP

First gossip: Why did they separate?

Second gossip: Nobody knows.

First gossip: Oh, how terrible.

———

Minister: The topic for this morning's message is gossip. Immediately following the message we will sing the hymn, "I Love to Tell the Story."

———

Gossip is mouth-to-mouth recitation.

Gossip is letting the chat out of the bag.

Gossip is the ability to know how to keep a secret…in circulation.

GROSS

Q: Why should the number 288 never be mentioned in polite company?

A: Because it is too gross.

GRUESOME

A little taller than before.

GUMDROP

A receptacle for used chewing gum.

HABITS

Bad habits are like a comfortable bed—
easy to get into but hard to get out of.

Banana split personality

"I get separation anxiety when my food is gone."

HALF

During a seminary class, the lesson centered on the problem of King Herod offering up half his kingdom for the dancing of the daughter of Herodias.

"Now, what if you had this problem and you made the offer of anything she wanted, and the girl came to you asking for the head of John the Baptist, and you didn't want to give her the head of John. What would you do?" asked the professor.

Soon a hand was raised, "I'd tell her," said one student, "that the head of John the Baptist was not in the half of the kingdom I was offering to her."

HALF-WIT

Person who spends half his time thinking up wisecracks and definitions.

HEARING AID

Moe: This hearing aid I bought is the most expensive one on the market. It cost $2,500.

Joe: What kind is it?

Moe: A half-past-four.

HICKORY DICKORY DOCK

Hickory dickory dock,

The elephant ran up the clock.

The clock is now being repaired.

HOG CALLER

A local pastor joined a community service club, and the members thought they would have some fun with him. Under his name on the badge they printed "hog caller" as his occupation.

There was big fanfare as the badge was presented. The pastor responded by saying: "I usually am called 'Shepherd of the Sheep' but you know your people better than I do."

HOW MANY NEEDED?

How many actors does it take to change a light bulb?

Fifteen. One to change it, and 14 to say, "I could have done that."

———

How many doctors does it take to change a light bulb?

It depends on how much health insurance the light bulb has.

———

How many social scientists does it take to change a light bulb?

None. Social scientists don't change light bulbs. They search for the root cause of the light bulb's failure.

———

How many bureaucrats does it take to change a light bulb?

Two. One to assure us that everything is being done to deal with the problem, and the other to screw a new light bulb into the hot water faucet.

———

"It's Cecelia's…she makes a mean meatloaf."

"Hugging is Natalie's way of showing
the cat the Heimlich maneuver."

How many paranoids does it take to change a light bulb?

Who wants to know?

———

How many optimists does it take to change a light bulb?

None. They believe the power will be back on in a minute.

———

How many circus performers does it take to change a light bulb?

Four. One to change the bulb and three to shout out, "Ta-daaaaa!"

———

How many country music singers does it take to change a light bulb?

Two. One to change it…and one to sing about how much she's going to miss the old bulb.

———

How many gorillas does it take to change a light bulb?

One, but you will need lots and lots of light bulbs.

YOU KNOW YOU'RE GETTING OLDER WHEN...

- You're at the stage of life where happy hour is a nap.
- You get winded playing checkers.
- You join a health club and don't go.
- You decide to procrastinate but then never get around to it.

- Your mind makes contracts that your body can't meet.
- You have too much room in the house and not enough in the medicine cabinet.

HUCK

Finn and Huck were friends. Finn up and died. No one was worried, however. They said: "Huck'll bury Finn."

HUSBAND

A wife complained to her neighbor, "He mixes everything up. I called him before he left work and asked him to pick up a sack of potatoes on the way home. I'll bet he even mixes that up."

Minutes later, the husband rushed into the house. "Look what I found!" he exclaimed, dropping a large bag of money on the table.

"See," said the wife to the neighbor. "I told you he'd get it mixed up."

HIGH HEELS

The invention of a girl who had been kissed on the forehead too many times.

HYPOCRITICAL

Anyone who tells you your hips are getting too big.

IGNORANCE

Fred: They say that ignorance is bliss.

Ted: Then you should be the happiest man in the world!

"Good!"

Saxaphobia

ILLEGAL

A sick bird.

IMPRESSIVE

The bank director was impressed by the young trainee's facility with figures. He said, "Where did you learn your math?"

The trainee answered, "Yale."

"Yale," said the bank director. "That is very good! And what is your name?"

"Yerry Yackson."

INADMISSIBLE

Judge: Did you see the shot that was fired?

Witness: I only heard it.

Judge: That is pure hearsay and inadmissible as evidence.

As the witness left the stand with his back turned to the judge, he laughed out loud. At once the judge called him back and was about to hold him in contempt of court.

Witness: Did you see me laugh?

Judge: No, but I heard you.

Witness: Isn't that the same kind of inadmissible evidence, Judge?

INCOME TAX

Don't be surprised if your next income tax form is simplified to contain only four lines?

1. What was your income last year?
2. What were your expenses?
3. How much do you have left?
4. Send it in.

IN FRONT

When you get kicked from the rear it means you're in front.

INSANITY

The statistics on sanity are that one out of every four Americans is suffering from some form of mental illness. Think of your three best friends. If they're okay, you're the one.

INTENSE

Where campers sleep.

INTERRUPT

Member to pastor at the end of the morning service: "Pastor, you were really good this morning! You interrupted my thoughts at least half a dozen times!"

Dr. Hamm on rye. Hold the Mayo.

"The glasses should help. Either way,
always look before you leap."

IRON ORE

An oar you can hardly row with.

JANITOR

Did you hear about the church janitor who also played the piano on Sunday? He watched his keys and pews.

JELLY

Q: Where do jellyfish get their jelly?

A: From ocean currents.

JELLYFISH

Q: What kind of fish do you eat with peanut butter?

A: Jellyfish.

JOY OF MOTHERHOOD

What a woman experiences when all the kids are in bed.

JULIUS CAESAR

Shakespeare: I've written a good play, but I think the title is too long.

Friend: What is the title?

Shakespeare: I call it, "Julius, Grab the Girl Quickly Before She Gets Away."

Friend: Why not just call it, "Julius Caesar"?

JUMP

Q: How can you jump off a 50-foot ladder and not get hurt?

A: Jump off the first step.

JUNK

Something you keep ten years and then throw
away two weeks before you need it.

KAZOO

The sound of a sneeze.

KINGDOM

A king who isn't very bright.

KNAPSACK

A sleeping bag.

KNOCK, KNOCK

Knock, knock.

Who's there?

Amos.

Amos who?

A mosquito bit me.

Knock, knock.

Who's there?

Andy.

Andy who?

And he bit me again.

LARGE PILL

A patient limped into the doctor's office. The doctor handed the patient a large pill. Just then his nurse asked him some questions. The patient limped over to the sink and choked down the pill. Then the doctor returned with a bucket and said, "Now drop the pill in the bucket and we will soak your foot."

LAUGH

From the moment I picked up your joke book
until I laid it down, I was convulsed with
laughter. Someday I intend on reading it.

LAUGHING

Two men went to the train station with a friend. The train was late, so they sat down for a cup of coffee. They talked and drank and forgot about the train. Suddenly they heard the last announcement about the departing train. They all got up and started running. They ran down the tracks as the train was pulling out of the station. Two of the men made it to the last car and the third man was just not fast enough. The third man slowed to a stop and started laughing. An onlooker went up to the laughing man and said, "What are you laughing for? You just missed your train." "You're right," was the reply. "I did miss my train. What's funny is those two men came to see me off."

"Which path less traveled should I take?"

LAWN MOWER

The man in the repair shop said, "Here it is, Mr. Wilson. Your lawn-mower is now in perfect condition. Just one word of advice. Don't ever lend it to a neighbor."

"That's just the trouble," said Mr. Wilson. "I am the neighbor."

LECTURE

At a lecture series, a very poor speaker was on the platform. As he was speaking, people in the audience began to get up and leave. After about ten minutes there was only one man left. Finally the man stopped speaking and asked the man why he remained to the end. "I'm the next speaker," he replied.

LEND

It is better to give than to lend, and it costs about the same.

LIAR, LIAR, PANTS ON FIRE

- The check is in the mail.
- It won't hurt.
- I gave at the office.
- Come on, tell me. I promise I won't get angry.
- You don't look a day over 40.
- You don't need it in writing—you have my word.
- I'll call you later.
- It was delicious, but I couldn't eat another bite.
- It's supposed to make that noise.

- Your hair looks fine.
- You're lucky—this is the last one in stock.
- Don't worry, he's never bitten anyone before.
- All of our work is guaranteed.
- I'm on your side.
- You both must come again.

LIFE INSURANCE

The thing that keeps you poor all your life so you can die rich.

LION

A small man said to a large man, "If I were as big as you, I would go into the jungle, find me a big lion, and pull him limb from limb."

The big man replied, "There are some little lions in the jungle too. Let's see what you can do."

LOCOMOTIVE

A ridiculous reason for doing something.

LOVE

Q: What becomes of love triangles?

A: They turn into wreck tangles.

MATH SKILLS

If you want to teach your kids to count,
give them different allowances.

Embarrassing moments for scribes

MARRIAGE

A couple's happy married life almost went on the rocks because of the presence in the household of old Aunt Emma. For seven long years she lived with them, always crotchety, always demanding. Finally the old girl died.

On the way back from the cemetery, the husband confessed to his wife, "Darling, if I didn't love you so much, I don't think I would have put up with having your Aunt Emma in the house all those years."

His wife looked at him, aghast. "My Aunt Emma!" she cried. "I thought she was your Aunt Emma!"

———

Just because his wife crowns him doesn't
mean a man is king in his own house.

———

One night a wife found her husband standing over their baby's crib. Silently she watched him. As he stood looking down at the sleeping infant, she saw on his face a mixture of emotions: disbelief, doubt, delight, amazement, enchantment, skepticism.

Touched by this unusual display and the deep emotions it aroused, she slipped her arm around her husband, her eyes glistening.

"A penny for your thoughts," she said.

"It's amazing!" he replied. "I just can't see how anybody can make a crib like that for only $46.50."

———

Husband: Why do you want me to walk with you to put out the garbage?

Wife: So I can tell my friends that we go out once in a while.

Wife: I can't sleep, dear. I keep thinking there's a mouse under the bed.

Husband: Well, start thinking there's a cat under the bed and go to sleep.

MATHEMATICS

A Missouri farmer passed away and left 17 mules to his three sons. The instructions left in the will said that the oldest boy was to get one-half, the second eldest one-third, and the youngest one-ninth. The three sons, recognizing the difficulty of dividing 17 mules into these fractions, began to argue.

The uncle heard about the argument, hitched up his mule, and drove out to settle the matter. He added his mule to the 17, making it 18. The eldest son therefore got one-half or nine; the second got one-third or six; and the youngest got one-ninth or two. Adding up 9, 6, and 2 equals 17. The uncle having settled the argument, hitched up his mule and drove home.

MELLOW

A church soloist was delighted when one of the members spoke to him after church and said, "You have a very mellow voice."

The soloist went home and looked up the definition of "mellow" in his dictionary. He read: "Mellow...overripe and almost rotten."

"The Bible says, 'Be anxious for nothing.'
That's exactly what I'm doing!"

MEMBRANE

The part of your brain you remember with.

MIDDLE AGE

Middle age is that period when you are just as young as ever, but it takes a lot more effort.

MINISTER

The new minister stood at the church door greeting the members as they left the Sunday morning service. Most of the people were very generous in telling the new minister how they liked his message, except for one man who said, "That was a very dull and boring sermon, Pastor."

In a few minutes the same man appeared again in the line and said, "I didn't think you did any preparation of your message, Pastor."

Once again, the man appeared, this time muttering, "You really blew it. You didn't have a thing to say, Pastor."

Finally the minister could stand it no longer. He went over to one of the deacons and inquired about the man.

"Oh don't let that guy bother you," said the deacon. "All he does is go around repeating whatever he hears other people saying."

———

The minister of a large church asked the secretary to put his topic on the bulletin board so that everyone could see what his next Sunday's sermon would be. He said, "My topic is 'Are Ministers Cracking Up?'"

The secretary put up the following announcement: OUR MINISTER'S CRACKING UP.

MINISTERS

Thirteen ministers were on a flight to New York. When they came into a large storm, they told the stewardess to tell the pilot that everything would be okay because 13 ministers were on board.

Later the stewardess returned from the cockpit.

"What did the pilot say?" one preacher asked.

"He said he was glad to have 13 ministers aboard, but he would rather have four good engines."

MINOR OPERATION

One performed on somebody else.

MONDAYS

An awful way to spend one seventh of one's life.

"If you don't stop with the worry warts, you're gonna croak."

MONEY

A explorer was captured by some Spanish pirates. The captain told his interpreter to say to the explorer, "Tell him if he doesn't tell us where they have hidden all of their gold, we will burn both of his feet in the fire."

Through the interpreter the explorer responded, "I'd rather die than tell you where the gold is." With that they burned his feet in the fire.

The captain then told the interpreter to say, "Tell him that if he doesn't tell us where the gold is hidden, we will hang him from that noose on the tree over there."

The explorer again responded, "I'd rather die than tell you where the gold is." With that, they took him over to the tree and hung him until he could hardly breathe.

The pirate captain then ordered the explorer to be brought to him again. This time he said to the interpreter, "Tell him if he doesn't tell us where the gold is that we will skin him alive."

The explorer could stand it no longer and said, "The gold is hidden in a little cave just behind the large waterfall. The waterfall is one mile over the hill to the right."

The interpreter related the following to the captain, "He said that he would rather die than tell you where the gold is."

––––––––

Wife: I think you only married me because my daddy left me a lot of money.

Husband: That's not true. I didn't care who left you the money.

MONTH

Q: In what month do people talk the least?

A: February.

MORAL OF THE STORY

The owner of a filling station decided to get married. He happened to have a large room over his station. He invited all of the friends in the neighborhood. So many friends showed up that their combined weight caused the building to collapse.

Moral of the story: Never marry above your station.

MOTIVATION

A young man had a job with a company that required him to work very late at night. In going home after work, he found it was faster to walk through a cemetery near his home than to go another way. One night when he was very tired, he accidentally fell into a freshly dug grave.

At first he was not too concerned, but when he realized that he could not get out because the hole was too deep, he became somewhat hysterical. Finally, in complete exhaustion, he sat down in the corner of the grave and fell asleep.

Shortly thereafter another man decided to walk through the cemetery and happened to fall into the same grave. He too went through great effort to get out but could not. He then moved around the grave until he stepped on the first man who was asleep. The first man woke up and shouted, *"You can't get out of here!"*

But he did.

MOZART

A married couple trying to live up to a snobbish lifestyle went to a party. The conversation turned to Mozart. "Absolutely brilliant, magnificent, a genius!"

The woman, wanting to join in the conversation, remarked casually, "Ah, Mozart. You're so right. I love him. Only this morning I saw him getting on the No. 5 bus going to Coney Island." There was a sudden hush, and everyone looked at her. Her husband was mortified. He pulled her away and whispered, "We're leaving right now. Get your coat and let's get out of here."

As they drove home, he kept muttering to himself. Finally his wife turned to him. "You're angry about something."

"Oh, really? You noticed?" He sneered. "I've never been so embarrassed in my life! You saw Mozart take the No. 5 bus to Coney Island? Don't you know the No.5 doesn't go to Coney Island?"

MUGWUMP

One who sits on a political fence with his mug
on one side and his wump on the other.

NATURAL SELECTION

Taking the largest piece.

NAUGHTY

Mother: Every time you're naughty, I get another gray hair.

Son: Wow, Mom, you must have been a terror when you were young... just look at Grandma.

"A person who spreads optimism
is *can*tagious."

NECESSITY

Almost any luxury you see in the home of a neighbor.

NET INCOME

The money a fisherman earns.

NEXT

A fellow went to a psychiatrist and said, "Doctor, I don't know what's wrong with me. Nobody wants to talk to me. My employees don't talk to me, my children don't talk to me, my wife doesn't talk to me. Why is it that nobody wants to talk to me?"

The psychiatrist said, "Next!"

NUMBERS

If the metric system ever takes over, we may have to do the following:

- A miss is as good as 1.6 kilometers.
- Put your best 0.3 of a meter forward.
- Spare the 5.03 meters and spoil the child.
- Twenty-eight grams of prevention is worth 453 grams of cure.
- Give a man 2.5 centimeters, and he'll take 1.6 kilometers.

OBSERVANT

Did you hear about the observant chap who
claims to have discovered the color of the
wind? He went out and found it blew.

OCTOPUS

A cat with only eight lives left.

OLD

You can tell you are getting old when:

- You sit in a rocking chair and can't get it going.
- You burn the midnight oil after 8:00 p.m.
- You look forward to a dull evening.
- Your knees buckle, and your belt won't.
- Your back goes out more than you do.
- You decide to procrastinate and never get around to it.
- You walk with your head held high, trying to get used to your bifocals.
- You sink your teeth into a steak, and they stay there.

OLD AGE

Old age comes when your memory grows
shorter and your stories longer.

———

Old age is when you finally know all the
answers but can't remember the questions.

———

Bun Hur

"I'm working on strengthening my core."

I never lie about my age. I just tell people I'm as old as my wife—and then I lie about her age.

———

I was always told to respect my elders. It's just getting harder and harder to find one.

———

People who knew him 40 years ago say he still looks like he looked then…old.

———

The greatest problem about old age is the fear that it may go on too long.

A.J.P. TAYLOR

———

Two little girls were talking: "My grandmother is always complaining about how awful it feels to be old," said the first one. The other responded, "Mine too. I guess those wrinkles hurt a lot."

———

These days, I spend a lot of time thinking about the hereafter. I go to get something and then wonder what I'm here after.

———

I decided to take an aerobics class for seniors. I bent and twisted, gyrated, jumped up and down, and perspired for more than an hour. But by the time I got my tights on, the class was over.

OLD BORE

A tired minister was at home resting. But through the window he saw a woman approaching his door. She was one of those too-talkative people, and he was not eager to talk with her. He said to his wife: "I'll just duck upstairs and wait until she goes away."

An hour passed, and then he tiptoed to the stair landing and listened. Not a sound. He was very pleased, so he started calling loudly to his wife, "Well, my dear, did you get rid of that old bore at last?"

The next moment he heard the voice of the same woman caller, and she couldn't possibly have missed hearing him. Two steps down, he saw them both staring up at him. It seemed truly a crisis moment.

The quick-thinking minister's wife answered, "Yes, dear, she went away more than an hour ago. But Mrs. Jones has come to call in the meantime, and I'm sure you'll be glad to greet her."

OLD NATURE

A man was taken to court for stealing an item from a store. The man said to the judge, "Your Honor, I'm a Christian. I've become a new man. But I have an old nature also. It was not my new man who did wrong. It was my old man."

The judge responded, "Since it was the old man that broke the law, we'll sentence him to 60 days in jail. And since the new man was an accomplice in the theft, we'll give him 30 days also. I therefore sentence you both to 90 days in jail."

"And for your depression, Ms. Goodall,
I'm prescribing a barrel of monkeys."

"I don't get enough exercise? Are you saying
brushing my teeth isn't exercise?"

OPERATION

Q: What is the greatest surgical operation on record?

A: Lancing Michigan.

OPPOSITES

Your Problem	*My Situation*
When you get angry, it is because you are ill-tempered.	It just happens that my nerves are bothering me.
When you don't like someone, it is because you are prejudiced.	I happen to be a good judge of human nature.
When you compliment some-one, it is because you use flattery.	I only encourage folks.
When you take a long time to do a job, it is because you are unbearably slow and pokey.	When I take a long time, it is because I believe in quality workmanship.
When you spend your paycheck in 24 hours, it is because you are a spendthrift.	When I do, it is because I am generous.
When you stay in bed until 11 a.m., it is because you are a lazy good-for-nothing.	When I stay in bed a little longer, it is because I am totally exhausted.

OVEREATING

An activity that will make you thick to your stomach.

OXYMORONS

- Affordable housing
- Airline food
- Civil war
- Fun run
- Hot chili
- Living dead
- New classic
- Peace force
- Rap music
- Singles club
- Soft rock
- Student teacher
- Tax return

PARADISE

Two ivory cubes with dots all over them.

PASTOR

During the morning sermon, the pastor said, "If there is anyone here who doesn't believe in a personal devil, just come up and see me after the service."

"Somebody robbed the barbecue place.
I'm grilling the suspects now."

"Our bills are getting too high."

A pastor wired all his pews with electricity. One Sunday from the pulpit he said, "All who will give $100 toward the new building, stand up." He touched a button and 20 people sprang up.

"Fine, fine," the preacher beamed. "Now all who will give $500, stand up." He touched another button and 20 more jumped to their feet.

"Excellent," he shouted. "Now all who will give $1000, stand up." He threw the master switch and electrocuted 15 deacons.

———

A pastor, burdened by the importance of his work, went into the sanctuary to pray. Falling to his knees, he lamented, "O Lord, I am nothing! I am nothing!"

The minister of education passed by, and overhearing the prayer, was moved to join the pastor on his knees. Shortly he too was crying aloud, "O Lord, I too am nothing. I am nothing."

The janitor of the church, awed by the sight of two men praying, joined them, crying, "O Lord, I also am nothing. I am nothing."

At this, the minister of education nudged the pastor and said, "Now look who thinks he's nothing!"

PENNY PINCHER

Years ago a Scotsman was arguing with a conductor as to whether the fare was 25 or 50 cents. Finally the disgusted conductor picked up the Scot's suitcase and tossed it off the train just as they passed over a bridge. It landed with a splash.

"Mon," screamed the Scot, "it isn't enough to try to overcharge me, but now you try to drown my little boy!"

PIG IRON

An iron for smoothing wrinkles off pigs.

PIG TOES

In a small town, the farmers of the community had gotten together to discuss some important issues. About midway through the meeting, a wife of one of the farmers stood up and spoke her piece. One old farmer stood up and said, "What does she know about anything? I would like to ask her if she knows how many toes a pig has."

Quick as a flash, the woman replied, "Take off your boots, man, and count them!"

PLEASURE TRIP

First Mother: I just came back from a pleasure trip.

Second Mother: Where did you go?

First Mother: I drove my kids to camp.

POLICE HELICOPTER

The whirlybird that catches the worm.

POPPED EYES

A man sought medical aid because he had popped eyes and a ringing in the ears. A doctor looked him over and suggested removal of his tonsils. The operation resulted in no improvement, so the patient consulted another doctor who suggested removal of his teeth. The teeth were extracted, but still the man's eyes popped and the ringing in his ears continued.

A third doctor told him bluntly, "You've got six months to live." In that event, the doomed man decided he'd treat himself right while he could. He bought a flashy car, hired a chauffeur, had the best tailor in town to make him 30 suits, and decided even his shirts would be made-to-order.

"Okay," said the shirt maker, "let's get your measurement. Hmmm, 34 sleeve, 16 collar—"

"Fifteen," the man said.

"Sixteen collar," the shirt maker repeated, measuring again.

"But I've always worn a 15 collar," said the man.

"Listen," the shirt maker said, "I'm warning you. You keep on wearing a 15 collar and your eyes will pop and you'll have ringing in your ears."

POTATO CHIPS

Q: What do you call a monkey that sells potato chips?

A: A chipmonk.

PRAY

An ocean liner was sinking, and the captain yelled: "Does anybody know how to pray?"

A minister on board said, "I do."

"Good," said the captain. "You start praying. The rest of us will put on the life belts. We are one belt short."

"Ah, yes...here's what we want."

PRAYER

A farmer was in town at noon and went into a restaurant for a hamburger and french fries. When he was served, he quietly bowed his head and gave the Lord thanks for his food.

Some rough-looking fellows at the next table saw him and thought they would give him a hard time. One of them called out, "Hey, farmer, does everyone do that where you live?"

"No, son," answered the farmer, "the pigs and donkeys don't."

PREACHERS

Preacher: A lot of people must be sick with colds. There was sure a lot of coughing during my sermon this morning.

Deacon: Those were time signals.

PREPARE

A salesman was assigned to secure an important client but failed in his mission. He wrote back to his secretary and asked her to break the news indirectly to his boss. His note read, "Failed in securing client, prepare the boss."

He received the following note from his secretary: "The boss is prepared…prepare yourself."

PRESS THE BUTTON

A young businessman was leaving his job after working late. On the way out he happened to run into his boss, who was standing in front of a shredder with a piece of paper in his hand.

"Can you help me?" asked the CEO. "I have this very sensitive and important document here, and my secretary has gone for the night. Can you make this thing work for me?"

"Certainly," said the young man, wanting to assist his boss. He turned on the machine, inserted the paper, and pressed the start button.

"Excellent, excellent!" Said the CEO as he watched the paper disappear inside the machine. "I just need one copy."

PRIDE

Did you hear about the man who had a gold tooth that was the pride of his life? He got in a fight the other day, and someone hit him in the mouth. He had to swallow his pride.

PROFANE

A pastor and one of his parishioners were playing golf at a local country club. It was a very close match. At the last hole, the pastor teed up, addressed the ball, and swung his driver with great force. The ball stubbornly rolled off the tee and settled slowly some 12 feet away instead of sailing down the fairway.

The clergyman frowned, glared after the ball, and bit his lip but said nothing.

His opponent regarded him for a moment and sighed, "Pastor, that is the most profane silence I have ever heard!"

"I didn't really start applying myself
seriously until around the eighth life."

"What a slobster!"

PSYCHIATRIST

Patient: I always feel that I'm covered in gold paint, Doctor.

Psychiatrist: Oh, that's just your gilt complex.

———

Patient: Doctor, I think everyone tries to take advantage of me.

Psychiatrist: That's silly. It's a perfectly normal feeling.

Patient: Is it really? Thanks for your help, Doctor. How much do I owe you?

Psychiatrist: How much do you have?

———

Psychiatrist: Mr. Strange, I understand your problem is that you constantly contradict people. Right?

Patient: Wrong.

Psychiatrist: I must be mistaken then.

Patient: You are not.

Psychiatrist: Oh, I get it. You're contradicting everything I say.

Patient: That's ridiculous.

Psychiatrist: I see. Then you're perfectly sane.

Patient: Ha! I'm as crazy as a loon.

Psychiatrist: Ah, we're finally making some progress.

———

Sign outside psychiatrist's office: "Guaranteed Satisfaction or Your Mania Back."

A patient explained to the psychiatrist that he was haunted by visions of his departed relatives.

Patient: These ghosts are perched on the tops of fence posts around my garden every night. They just sit there and watch me and watch me and watch me. What can I do?

Psychiatrist: That's easy—just sharpen the tops of the posts.

A psychiatrist is someone who asks you a lot of expensive questions that your spouse asks you for free.

PUPS

A minister preached a very short sermon. He explained, "My dog got into my office and chewed up some of my notes."

At the close of the service a visitor approached the pastor. "If your dog ever has pups, please let my pastor have one of them."

PUTT

"You think so much of your old golf game you don't even remember when we were married."

"Of course I do, my dear. It was the day I sank that 30-foot putt."

QUACK

A doctor who ducks the law.

QUADRUPLETS

Four crying out loud.

RAIN

Q: When rain falls, does it ever get up again?

A: Yes, in dew time.

RATTAN

What a rat gets while vacationing in Florida.

REPETITION

A professor of English was trying to drum into his class the importance of a large vocabulary.

"I assure you," he said, "if you repeat a word ten or twelve times, it will be yours forever."

In the back of the room a girl took a deep breath, closed her eyes, and whispered, "Richard, Richard, Richard…"

"Are there any openings in the labor department?"

RESTITUTION

A home for chronically exhausted people.

REVENGE

Did you hear about the man who burned the farmer's sugarcane field? He wanted sweet revenge.

ROSE

Carl: What's that you have in your buttonhole?

Earl: Why, that's a chrysanthemum.

Carl: It looks like a rose to me.

Earl: Nope, you're wrong. It's a chrysanthemum.

Carl: Spell it.

Earl: K-r-i-s...by golly, that is a rose.

RUBBER BAND

In the bank one day, a little boy suddenly called out at the top of his voice, "Did anyone drop a roll of bills with a rubber band around it?"

Several people at different tellers' windows answered, "I did!"

"Well, I just now found the rubber band," said the boy.

RULE THE WORLD

Husband: I know you're having a lot of trouble with the baby, dear, but keep in mind, "The hand that rocks the cradle is the hand that rules the world."

Wife: Well, in that case, would you mind taking over the world while I go shopping?

SAME MEDICINE

Patient: What are your fees, Doctor?

Doctor: I charge ten dollars for the first visit and five dollars for the second visit.

Patient: Well, Doctor, it's nice to see you again! What should I do?

Doctor: Take the same medicine I gave you last time.

SANTA CLAUS

A person who does not come through the chimney but through a large hole in the pocketbook.

"Fair warning, Hargraves—
we do everything by the book."

SCHOOL

A mother was having a hard time getting her son to attend school one morning. "Nobody likes me at school," said the son. "The teachers don't, and the kids don't. The superintendent wants to transfer me, the bus drivers hate me, the school board wants me to drop out, and the custodians have it in for me. I don't want to go."

"You've got to go," insisted the mother. "You're healthy. You've a lot to learn. You've got something to offer others. You're a leader. Besides, you're 49 years of age, you're the principal, and you've got to go to school."

———

Professor: Do you know the difference between ammonia and pneumonia?

Student: Sure. One comes in bottles and the other in chests.

SCREAM

Husband: Why do you weep and snuffle over a television program and the imaginary woes of people you have never met?

Wife: For the same reason you scream and yell when a man you don't know makes a touchdown.

SCREENS

An invention for keeping flies in the house.

SHOCK

A minister was asked to inform a man with a heart condition that he had just inherited a million dollars. Everyone was afraid the shock would cause a heart attack and the man would die.

The minister went to the man's house and said, "Joe what would you do if you inherited a million dollars?" Joe responded, "Well, Pastor, I think I would give half of it to the church."

And the minister fell over dead.

SHOES

A psychiatrist was trying to comfort a new patient who was terribly upset.

"You see, Doc," the patient explained, "my problem is that I like shoes much better than I like boots."

"Why, that's no problem," answered the doctor. "Most people like shoes better than boots."

The patient was elated, "That's neat, Doc. How do you like them, fried or scrambled?"

SISTERS

Father: Why did you put that frog in your sister's bed?

Jonny: Because I couldn't find any spiders.

SIX-YEAR-OLD

It isn't easy to be the parent of a six-year-old these days. However, it's a small price to pay to have someone around the house who understands computers.

SLEEP

A clothing manufacturer, worried that he couldn't sleep, was advised by his business associates to count sheep. Next day the man appeared more exhausted than ever. "Sure, I counted sheep," he told his associates. "I counted up to 20,000. Then I began figuring: Those 20,000 sheep would produce 80,000 pounds of wool—enough to make 30,000 yards of cloth. That would make 12,000 overcoats. Man! Who could sleep with an inventory like that?"

SPEECH

A speaker was having a little trouble getting started in his speech. All of a sudden someone from the audience shouted: "Tell 'em all you know. It will only take a minute."

"I'll tell 'em all we both know," shot back the speaker. "It won't take any longer."

SPEEDING

A minister was pulled over by a policeman for speeding. During the conversation the minister said, "Blessed are the merciful, for they shall obtain mercy." The policeman smiled, handed the minister a ticket, and said, "Go thou and sin no more."

SPONSOR

The longest word in the English language is the one that follows "and now a word from our sponsor…"

STAR

When an old TV star's show was canceled by the powers that be, a fan asked him, "Do you personally answer the hundreds of letters that come in every day demanding your program be renewed?" He answered disarmingly, "Goodness, no! I scarcely have time to write them!"

STOCKING

A jeweler watched as a huge truck pulled up in front of his store. The back came down and an elephant walked out. It broke one of the windows with its tusk and then, using the trunk like a vacuum cleaner, sucked up all the jewelry. The elephant then got back into the truck, which disappeared out of sight. When the jeweler finally regained his senses, he called the police. The detectives came, and he told them his story.

"Could you describe the elephant?"

"An elephant is an elephant. You see one you've seen them all. What do you mean, 'describe him?'" asked the jeweler.

"Well," said the policeman, "there are two kinds of elephants, African and Indian. The Indian elephant has smaller ears and is not as large as the African elephant."

The jeweler said, "I can't help you out; he had a stocking pulled over his head."

"What does it all mean?"

"A little something to hold you over
to the next sample table, sir?"

STORIES

Delivering a speech at a banquet on the night of his arrival in a large city, a visiting minister told several anecdotes he expected to repeat at meetings the next day. Because he wanted to use the jokes again, he requested the reporters to omit them from any accounts they might turn in to their newspapers. A cub reporter, commenting on the speech, ended his piece with the following: "The minister told a number of stories that cannot be published."

STRING

Q: How many balls of string would it take to reach the moon?

A: Only one, if it were long enough.

STUCCO

What you get when you sit on gummo.

SUE

A first-grader slipped in the hall of the school and sprained his ankle. His teacher, hurrying to console him, said, "Remember, Johnny, big boys don't cry."

"I'm not going to cry," snapped Johnny. "I'm going to sue."

SUN

"Did you hear about the chap who stays up all night figuring out where the sun went when it went down?"

"No, what happened?"

"It finally dawned on him."

SUGGESTION BOX

After examining the contents of the employees' suggestion box, the boss complained, "I wish they'd be more specific. What kind of kite? What lake?"

SUNDAY MESSAGE

First preacher: I think a pastor needs to study diligently for his Sunday morning message.

Second preacher: I disagree. Many times I have no idea what I am going to preach about, but I go into the pulpit and preach and think nothing of it.

First preacher: And you are quite right in thinking nothing of it. Your deacons have told me they share your opinion.

SWOLLEN

Doctor: Well, your leg is swollen, but I wouldn't worry about it.

Patient: No, and if your leg was swollen, I wouldn't worry about it either.

TAIL

Q: If a dog lost his tail, where would he get another one?

A: At the retail store, naturally.

"He loves to retweet."

"I always try to be the bigger person."

TAKEOUT

Husband: What's for supper?

Wife: Takeout.

Husband: What kind of takeout?

Wife: Me.

TALKING

Teacher: What do you call a person who keeps on talking when people are no longer interested?

Student: A teacher.

TAX COLLECTOR

Remember Matthew the tax collector?
They called him Levi for shorts.

TAXPAYERS

People who don't have to take a civil service
test to work for the government.

TENNIS

Discussing his tennis technique, a stout, bald man panted: "My brain immediately barks out a command to my body. 'Run forward, but fast,' it says. 'Start right now. Drop the ball gracefully over the net and then walk back slowly.'"

"And then what happens?" asked a friend.

"And then my body asks, 'Who, me?'"

TEXAN

A Texas rancher was visiting an Iowa farm. The Iowa farmer was justly proud of his 200 acres of rich, productive land.

"Is this your whole farm?" the Texan asked. "Why, back in Texas I get in my car at five in the morning, and I drive and drive all day. At dusk I just reach the other end of my ranch."

The Iowa farmer thought for a while and replied, "I used to have a car like that."

TEXAS

An Easterner was being driven by a rancher over a blistering and almost barren stretch of West Texas when a strange bird scurried in front of them. Asked what it was, the rancher replied, "That's a bird of paradise."

The stranger from the East rode on in silence for a moment, and then said, "Long way from home, isn't it?"

———

An ardent fisherman from Dallas made a trip to Bull Shoals Lake in Arkansas. After pulling in a six-pound largemouth bass, the Texan boasted to his native guide, "Why, in Texas we use that size for bait."

The Arkansan smiled, nodded appreciatively—and dropped the fish back into the lake.

THE ANSWER MAN

Q: What's more clever than speaking in several languages?

A: Keeping your mouth shut in one.

152

"I mean, the place went silent when I ordered decaf."

Habitat for Humidity

THOUGHTFUL

A very tight man was looking for a gift for a friend. Everything was too expensive except for a glass vase that had been broken, which he could purchase for almost nothing. He asked the store to send it, hoping his friend would think it had been broken in transit.

In due time he received an acknowledgement: "Thanks for the vase," it read. "It was so thoughtful of you to wrap each piece separately."

TIME

The shortest known unit is the time between the change of the traffic light and the honk from the car behind you.

———

Maybe people who are always on time aren't doing it to be courteous and polite. Maybe they're just mean people whose ambition in life is to make the rest of us feel guilty for being late.

TOASTMASTER

Member: Pastor, I would like you to act as master of ceremonies at a friend's burial service.

Pastor: Where is he going to be buried?

Member: Oh, he is going to be cremated.

Pastor: You don't want a master of ceremonies. What you need is a toastmaster.

TONGUE TWISTER

According to the *Guinness Book of World Records,* the toughest tongue-twister in the English language is this one:

The sixth sick sheik's sixth sheep's sick.

———

Bisquick, kiss quick.

———

Six slippery, sliding snakes.

———

The judge judged Judd.

———

Tim, the thin twin tinsmith.

———

Strange strategic statistics.

———

Toy boat.

TOOTHPASTE

Savings accounts are like toothpaste...easy to take out but hard to put back in.

"Alone, you're annoyed.
Together, you're a pair annoyed."

**"Let's begin by addressing your
delusional tendencies."**

TOP THIS

Bill: My dog swallowed a tapeworm and died by inches.

Bob: That's nothing—my dog crawled up in my bed and died by the foot.

Bill: I can beat that. I had a dog that went out of the house and died by the yard.

———

The following conversation was overheard at a party attended by high society people:

"My ancestry goes all the way back to Alexander the Great," said one lady. She then turned to a second lady and said, "And how far does your family go back?"

"I don't know," she replied. "All of our records were lost in the Flood."

TULIPS

The standard number of lips assigned to each person.

UNISON

An only male child.

UNTOLD WEALTH

That which does not appear on income tax returns.

"I'm puzzled."

UNTOUCHABLES

People as broke as you are.

VANGUARD

A person who protects trucks.

VENTRILOQUIST

A person who talks to himself for a living.

VIOLIN

An instrument for musicians who like to fiddle around.

WEIGHT

It's reported that there are 160 million overweight people in the United States. That is a round figure, of course.

WHAT'S IN A NAME?

What do you call a man with leaves in his ear?
Russell!

What do you call a man with a crane on his head?
Derek!

What do you call a man with black-and-blue marks on his head?
Bruce!

What do you call a woman with a breeze on her head?
Gail!

What do you call a man with a kilt on his head?
Scott!

What do you call a man with a legal document on his head?
Will!

What do you call a woman with a tortoise on her head?
Shelley.

What do you call a man with a steamroller on his head?
Dead!

WILL

A dead giveaway.

———

Patient: You have been a great doctor. I want to leave you something in my will rather than insulting you by paying my bill.

Doctor: That's great! By the way, let me have the prescription I just gave you. I want to make a slight change in it.

WORK

An unpopular way of earning money.

———

"Are you selfie-medicating again?"

A sportsman went to a hunting lodge and bagged a record number of birds, aided by a dog named Salesman. Next year he returned and asked for Salesman again. "The hound ain't no durn good now," the handler said.

"What happened!" cried the sportsman. "Was he injured?"

"No. Some fool came down here and called him 'Sales Manager' all week instead of Salesman. Now all he does is sit on his tail and bark."

———

The only man who ever got all his work done
by Friday was Robinson Crusoe.

———

If lawyers are disbarred and ministers unfrocked, perhaps electricians get delighted…Far Eastern diplomats disoriented…cashiers distilled…alpine climbers dismounted…piano tuners unstrung…orchestra leaders disbanded…artists' models deposed…cooks deranged…nudists redressed…office clerks defiled…dressmakers unbiased.

WORK VERSUS PRISON

In prison you spend most of your time in an 8 x 10 cell.
At work you spend most of your time in a 6 x 8 cubicle.

In prison you get three meals a day.
At work you get a break for only one meal, and you have to pay for it.

In prison you get time off for good behavior.
At work you get rewarded for good behavior with more work.

"Let the healing begin."

In prison a guard locks and unlocks all the doors for you.
At work you must carry around a security card and unlock and open all the doors yourself.

In prison you can watch television and play games.
At work you get fired for watching television and playing games.

In prison you have your own toilet.
At work you have to share.

In prison they allow family and friends to visit.
At work you cannot even speak to family and friends.

In prison you have unlimited time to read e-mail jokes.
At work you get fired if you get caught spending time on personal e-mail.

WORLD'S BEST AFTER-DINNER SPEECH

Waiter, give me both checks.

X-RAY

Belly vision.

———

A silence with an exclamation mark.

———

A silent shout.

"Am I addicted to my smart phone?
I don't know—let me ask Siri."

YES

Husband: Honey, will you still love me after I put on a few pounds?

Wife: Yes, I do.

———

Wife: Will you still love me when I'm old and feeble?

Husband: Of course I do.

ZANZIBAR

Ben: You know something? Between my father and me, we know everything.

Len: Oh, yeah? So tell me—where's Zanzibar?

Ben: Ask my father. That's one of the things he knows.

ZINC

What will happen to you if you don't know how to zwim.

ZOO

A place where animals look at silly people.

ABOUT THE AUTHOR

Bob Phillips, master compiler of inspirational verses, Scripture references, and quotes on the lighter, humorous side of life, has written over a hundred books with combined sales of more than 11 million copies. Bob also serves as executive director emeritus for Hume Lake Christian Camps and is a licensed family counselor in California.

ABOUT THE ARTIST

Jonny Hawkins is a full-time cartoonist whose work has appeared in more than 600 publications. He also creates five themed Cartoon-a-Day calendars each year. Jonny and his wife, Carissa, have three children and live in Michigan.

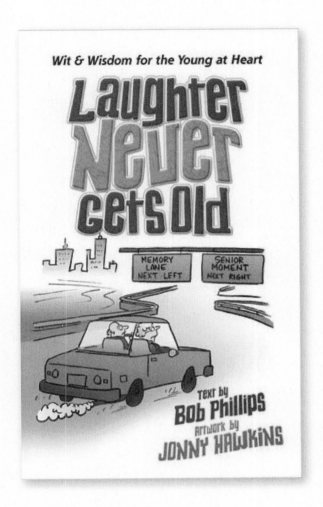

Wit & Wisdom for the Young at Heart

Laughter Never Gets Old

MEMORY LANE NEXT LEFT

SENIOR MOMENT NEXT RIGHT

Text by
Bob Phillips

Artwork by
JONNY HAWKINS

LAUGHTER NEVER GETS OLD

What's the secret to aging gracefully? It just might be a healthy sense of humor. Living well in the "third third of life" includes the ability to not take yourself too seriously. These jokes, brief stories, and cartoons will help you keep an upbeat attitude as the years race by.

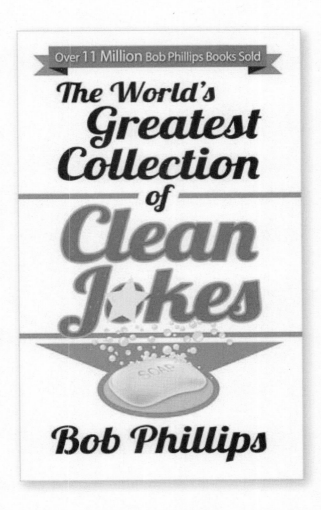

Over 11 Million Bob Phillips Books Sold

The World's Greatest Collection of Clean Jokes

Bob Phillips

THE WORLD'S GREATEST COLLECTION OF CLEAN JOKES

This top-selling collection of pure fun (over 510,000 copies sold) is back with a lively new cover to reach more readers eager to laugh. Puns, one-liners, jester-worthy jokes, and quirky quips will amaze and astound friends and family. Giggles are guaranteed as readers enjoy the crazy conversations and hilarious observations.

OVER THE HILL AND ON A ROLL

After selling more than 300,000 copies, *Over the Hill and on a Roll* gets a well-deserved face lift. The jokes never get old, even if readers do! They'll laugh at funny insights, memory challenges, and clever quizzes created by bestselling jokester Bob Phillips. The perfect birthday, retirement, or friendship gift.

To learn more about Harvest House books and
to read sample chapters, visit our website:

www.harvesthousepublishers.com

HARVEST HOUSE PUBLISHERS
EUGENE, OREGON